Copyright @ 2019 Kate Riley
All Rights Reserved

This book is unofficial and unauthorized. Product name, logos, brand and other trademarks featured or referred to in this publication are the property of J.K Rowling and Warner Bros, respective trademark holders and are not affiliated with this publication. The information in this book is meant for educational and entertainment purposes only. It is not authorized, approved, licensed or endorsed by Harry Potter Series' publisher and any other licensees or affiliates.

The content and information contained in this book have been compiled from sources deemed reliable, and they are accurate to the best of the Author's knowledge, information, and belief. Although the author and publisher have made every effort to ensure that the information presented in this book was correct at the present time, the author and publisher do not assume and hereby disclaim any liability to any party for any loss, damage, or disruption caused by errors or omissions, whether such errors or omission result from negligence, accident and any other cause.

ISBN: 9781650769950

MY Harry Potter OBSESSION IS A BIT Riddikulus

Content

Some fun techniques -5

Some Lingos -6

How to use this recipe book -7

Hot Butterbeer Rum Cocktail -8

Chocolate Frog Cocktail 10

Platform 9 ¾ beer -12

2 Hogwart Express Steampunk Cocktails -14

Divination Witches Brew Cocktail -16

Unicorn Silver Blood -18

Firebolt Broomstick Cocktail -20

Ron Weasly Sour Cocktail -22

Black Magic Cocktail -23

Pumkin Creamy Cocktail -24

Golden Snitch Cocktail -26

Dumbledore Cocktail -28

Phoenix's Tear Cocktail -30

Forbidden Forest Cocktail -32

Goblet of Fire Cocktail -34

Felix Felicis (Liquid Luck) -36

Flaming Dragon Cocktail -38

Sirius Black Cocktail -40

Content

Hermione Sunrise Cocktail -42

Bellatrix Cocktail -44

Dobby The Happy Elf Cocktail -46

Firewhisky Cocktail -48

Chocolatini Wolfbane Cocktail -50

Lumos Cocktail -51

PolyJuice Potion Punch -52

Pink Tonk Warrior Gin -55

Harry's Scar Cocktail -56

Alastor Moody Scottish Cocktail 58

Amortentia Potion Cocktail -60

Veritaserum Cocktail -62

Expecto Patronum Cocktail -64

Avada Bombastic Cocktail -66

Alohomora Cocktail -68

Gillywater Cocktail -70

Gryffindor Lion Cocktail -72

Ravenclaw Cocktail -74

Slytherin Cocktail -76

Hufflepuff Brew Party Cocktail -78

Quidditch Worldcup Cocktail -79

Some Fun techniques

Rimming: Use plate or shallow bowl of water, honey, syrup, lime juice or lemon juice then dip in the your glass'rim. Or you could cut a lime or lemon wedge rub the rim with it; it's totally up to you. Next, you need to evenly dip the rim into whatever you're rimming the glass with.

Layering: "Float" ingredients on top of one another to create cool layers. In this book, we use layering for creating the flaming cocktails.

Mudding: Gently press down and give a half-turn of the muddler. Release and continue this motion about four to six turns until the ingredients are sufficiently muddled. Add the other ingredients according to the recipe's recommendation.

Some Lingos

- ➢ **Dash and Splash:** *The smallest measurements found in a bar.. Technically, a dash is 1/32 of an ounce, but The exact measurement of either a dash or a splash is not important.*

- ➢ **Garnish:** *Often a fruit such as a cherry or an orange slice, a garnish is used to adorn a drink and add to its visual appeal. Some garnishes also bring in hints of flavor.*

- ➢ **Liquor and a liqueur**. *All liqueurs are a type of liquor, but not all liquors are liqueurs.*

- **Liquors** *are distilled spirits, meaning that a liquor is any alcoholic beverage that has been distilled. This includes* **the six base distilled spirits** *(Vodka, Gin, Rum, Brandy, Tequila, Whiskey) as well as sweetened liqueurs. If it has gone through a still and comes out with a high alcohol content, it is a liquor.*

- **Liqueurs** *are sweetened distilled spirits. It is a subcategory of liquors and this is where many drinks get their signature flavors.*

- ➢ **One part** *is any equal part. One part will become your base or foundation measurement and you will adjust the other ingredients to maintain the ratio. The key is to first decide what 1 part equals for that particular recipe.*

How to Use This Recipe Book?

Take in as much as you like at a time. Come back to review something or to study a topic a bit further. It's a crash course in mixing drinks and there is a lot of information to take in. At the end of this book, you will find blank recipe template pages that you and write down your own recipes. Take your time and enjoy!

Measurement units
oz: US Fluid Ounce
1 oz= 2 table Spoon (2 tbsp)
1 oz≈ 29.57 ml
Tsp: Teaspoon, Tsbp: Tablespoon
1 Tablespoon= 3 Teaspoon

Hot Butterbeer Rum Cocktail

This is by far the best "authentic" butter beer/hot buttered rum. You will regret not adding this Hot Butterbeer Rum Cocktail in your feast menu.

Ingredients

6 cups water
12 oz. (2 cans) cream soda
1 cup brown sugar
1/2 cup unsalted butter
1/2 cup butterscotch syrup, divided
3 cinnamon sticks
1 tsp. vanilla
1/2 tsp. salt
2 cups spiced rum

For garnishing:
Whipped cream, Gold sanding sugar

Servings: 8-10 Drinks

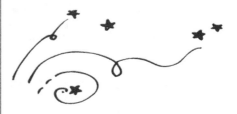

Instructions

Step 1: In Crock-Pot, combine water, cream soda, sugar, butter, 1/4 cup butterscotch, cinnamon sticks, vanilla and salt. Cover and cook on low for 3 to 3 and a half hours, until warm and butter is melted. Remove lid and stir in rum.

Step 2: Pour remaining butterscotch syrup onto a shallow plate. Dip rims of mugs in syrup before filling with butter beer. Top with whipped cream, sprinkle with sanding sugar, and serve.

Chocolate Frog Cocktail

Chocolate frogs are a very popular sweet made from chocolate in the form of a frog. The frogs are made of seventy percent Croakoa. Presumably, this substance is what allows them to act like an actual frog. In Harry, Ron, and Hermione first year at Hogwarts, The Chocolate Frog collectible cards enabled them to ascertain the identity of Nicolas Flamel through Professor Dumbledore's chocolate card.

A Chocolate Frog Cocktail is a fantastic way to enjoy chocolate and tequila in a single glass. Both tequila and orange juice are natural companions to chocolate. It goes beyond simply drinking spiked chocolate by adding just a hint of orange and lime.

Ingredients

1 cup ice
2 ounces blanco tequila
1 ounce chocolate liqueur
1 ounce cream (or half and half)
Splash orange juice (fresh)
Splash lime juice (fresh)
Dash chocolate bitters
Garnish: sugar and cocoa powder (for rim), shaved chocolate
Servings: 1 Drink

Tips

-Five or six average-sized ice cubes is equivalent to 1 cup of ice. Add these first to ensure the blender's blades chop them up quickly.
-For the chocolate liqueur, indulge with the creamiest, most chocolatey spirit that you can find.

Instructions

Rim: mix equal parts of sugar and cocoa powder in a small dish. Then wet the rim with a piece of citrus fruit by running it around the edge. Roll the wet rim in the cocoa sugar to get an even coat all the way around. Tap off any excess.

In a blender, add the ice, tequila, chocolate liqueur, cream, and bitters. Squeeze in a splash each of orange and lime juices. Blend until smooth.

Pour into the prepared glass. Top with chocolate shavings, serve and enjoy!

*** This margarita can also be shaken using the same ingredients, except for the ice.

PLATFORM 9 ¾ BEER

Platform 9¾)is a platform at King's Cross Station in London. In order to catch the Hogwarts Express, Harry and his friends get to the platform by dashing through a brick wall between platforms 9 and 10. At King's Cross, platforms 9 and 10 are separated by tracks, but you can find a platform 9¾ on the wall in the station concourse.

This cocktail recipe is dedicated to those of you feeling adventurous and want to start journey to Hogwarts. Are you ready? Use a pint or a bit larger glass. Check again your luggage trolley, you are off to start your magical trip and start making Platform 9 ¾ Beer now!

Ingredients

Mexican lager beer (Modelo or Dos Equis Ambar
Clamato juice (or tomato juice or homemade clam juice)
3-4 splashes hot sauce
2 splashes of Worcestershire sauce
2 splashes of Maggi sauce (or soy sauce)
Juice of one lime;
Chili lime seasoning (or salt) for the rim
Ice cubes (note: be aware not to watering down the drink)

Serving: 1 drink

Instructions

- If you are making clamato juice mix tomato juice and clam juice in 3:1 ratio, taste and add a bit more clam juice if needed. Chill.
- Take about a tablespoon of chili lime seasoning (or salt) and sprinkle it on a small plate. Rub a slice of lime around the rim of the glass and then press the rim in the chili lime seasoning.
- Fill the glass about ¼ to ⅓ with the Clamato juice. Add the hot sauce, the lime juice, the Worcestershire sauce, and the soy sauce. If you used Tajín to salt the rim, pour any excess from the plate into the glass.
- Fill the rest with cold beer.
- Garnish with a slice of lime

2 Hogwart Express Steampunk Cockltails

The Hogwarts Express is the name of the train that makes a run between London, King's Cross Station Platform 9¾ and Hogsmeade Station. I would like to present two elicately balanced cocktail recipes that represents a vintage trend of Hogwart Express.

Recipe 1

Ingredients

2 oz of Brandy
1 oz Applejack
1 oz sweet vermouth

Instruction

Pour into cocktail shaker with glass, stir well, and then strain into cocktail glass.

Ingredients

2 oz gin

0.75 oz lemon juice

0.75 oz of honey simple syrup

Add all ingredients to cocktail shaker, shake well and then strain into rocks glass. Garnish with lemon peel or twist.

Instructions

Add all ingredients to cocktail shaker, shake well and then strain into rocks glass. Garnish with lemon peel or twist.

Divination Witches Brew Cocktail

"Many witches and wizards, talented though they are in the area of loud bangs and smells and sudden disappearings, are yet unable to penetrate the veiled mysteries of the future." —Sybill Trelawney. Focus and use your Inner Eye to mix this Divination Witch Brew Cocktail.

This cocktail is so stunning. The Divination Witches Brew cocktail is a simple vodka based cocktail, that is delicious and just a little spooky but still with a sense of fun. You can use it as a long drink to serve up as a halloween cocktail.

Ingredients

6 cups orange juice
6 cups pomegranate juice
3 cups citrus vodka
Servings: 15 drinks

Notes

For a smaller batch:
2 parts orange juice
2 parts pomegranate juice
1 part vodka

Instructions

- Pour the orange juice, pomegranate juice, and vodka into your container of choice. I chose a 1 gallon glass jug.
- Shake or stir to combine, and serve.
- Refrigerate any unused portion in a sealed container for up to three days. It starts to taste strange after that.

Unicorn Silver Blood

The Unicorn, an iconic creature of magic, is a white horse with a horn sticking out of its head. These majestic equines possessed potent magical properties, with their tail hairs being designed by Garrick Ollivander as one of the "Supreme Cores". Unicorn blood is a thick, silvery magical substance that runs within a unicorn's veins. Lord Voldemort used to drink unicorn blood to sustain his life. "The blood of a unicorn will keep you alive, even if you are an inch from death, but at a terrible price. You have slain something pure and defenceless to save yourself, and you will have but a half-life, a cursed life, from the moment the blood touches your lips."

Bummer, huh? Luckily, you can enjoy this curse-free cocktail without worrying. Try out Unicorn Silver Blood Cocktail and have fun! No unicorns were harmed making this cocktail.

Ingredients

1 oz. Gin
1 oz. Vermouth (Dry)
1/8 oz. Maraschino Liqueur
1/4 oz of Orange Bitters
1/2 tsp Simple Syrup

Servings: 1 drink

Instructions

Pour all ingredients into a shaker with ice. Shake and strain into a chilled martini glass. Garnish: Cherry at the bottom.

Tips: Simple Syrup is a 1:1 sugar to water mix. Heated up until the sugar is dissolved. I make a batch a few times a year and keep in a jar in my fridge. Its great to have on hand for cocktails, lemonades etc.

A shaker a container used for mixing ingredients by shaking.

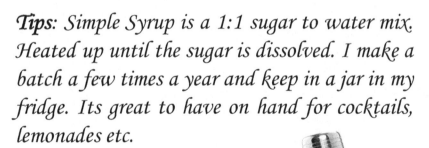

Firebolt Broomstick Cocktail

The Firebolt is a world-class broomstick. It was the fastest at the time of its production, and was released in 1993. The Firebolt is a costly broom and Harry Potter was one of the first to own one. We will use Fireball Whiskey, apples and cinnamon to complete this gorgeous recipe.

Ingredients

1.5 oz. Fireball Whiskey
1 cup Fresh Apple Cider
1 Splash Ginger Ale
1 Tbsp. Cinnamon and Sugar

Instructions

- Take a cocktail glass, dip the rim in a water on a small plate. Then dip into cinnamon and sugar poured onto a small plate. Spin glass to cover completely.
- Fill cinnamon and sugar rimmed glass with ice.
- Pour Fireball Whiskey over top of the ice.
- Add fresh apple cider over the Fireball.
- Finish with a splash of ginger ale. Stir and enjoy!

Ron Weasly Sour Cocktail

✯ ✩ ✩ ✩ ✯

This cocktail is simple and reliable in a pinch (just like Ron). All you have to do is shake up all the ingredients, pour it in a glass, and top it off with a cherry and an orange wedge. I like our Ron Weasly Sour thickened with egg white and a few dashes of aromatic bitters for a complementary spice.

Ingredients
2 oz Bourbon
3/4 oz Fresh lemon juice
1/2 oz Simple syrup
1/2 oz Egg white (optional)

Serving: 2-3 Drinks

Instructions
- Add all ingredients into a shaker with ice and shake.
- Strain into a coupe.
- Garnish with 3 dashes of Angostura bitters.

Black Magic Cocktail

Calling all beer and bourbon wizards! This is the midnight cocktail you'll be sipping from dawn till dusk.

Ingredients

3.5 oz Guinness draught
1.7 oz bourbon
2 tsp grenadine syrup
1 tbsp fresh lime juice
5 fresh blackberries
Lime wedges to garnish

Instructions

- Add the blackberries, bourbon, grenadine and lime juice into a cocktail shaker. Muddle the blackberries with a mudding spoon or the back of a rolling pin.

- Half fill the shaker with ice and shake hard for 30 seconds. Pour into a rocks glass filled with ice.

- Stir in the Guinness and garnish with a lime wedge and a couple of blackberries threaded on a toothpick.

Pumkin Creamy Cocktail

Pumpkin juice is a beverage made from pumpkins. Manufactured since 1837 by London Pumpkins & Sons, it is extremely popular in the wizarding world, particularly among the students at Hogwarts School of Witchcraft and Wizardry.

Pumpkin juice is usually served iced and it is available on the Hogwarts Express. Also it is drunk on any occasion, such as for breakfast, lunch, feasts, and other special events.

No wizarding gather-round-time should be complete without pumpkin juice. After all this time, pumpkin juice inspired cocktail is the one I like to make every time I want to relive some of the magic.

Ingredients

FOR THE DRINK

3 ounces 2 shot glasses good quality vodka

3 ounces 2 shot glasses pumpkin spice creamer

1.5 ounces 1 shot glass Kahlua

Whipped Cream and pumpkin pie spice for garnish

FOR THE RIM

1 teaspoon pumpkin pie spice

1 teaspoon sugar or sparkling sugar

3 tablespoons crushed graham crackers

Servings: 2 Drinks

Instructions

- Mix the ingredients for the rim together on a shallow plate. Dip the edge of two glasses in water and then dip into the graham mixture.

- Press to coat. Set the two glasses aside.

- Pour vodka, creamer, and kahlua into a large cocktail shaker filled with ice. Shake lightly until combined and cold.

- Pour into glasses and top with whipped cream and pumpkin pie spice

Golden Snitch Cocktail

The Golden Snitch(or the Snitch) is the third and smallest ball used in Quidditch. It is a walnut-sized gold-coloured sphere with silver wings flying around the Quidditch field at high speeds. The Seeker's goal is to catch the Snitch before the other team's seeker, worth one-hundred and fifty points. The game can only end when the Snitch has been caught. Harry Potter was the youngest Seeker in a century. Upon Albus Dumbledore's dealth, he left Harry the first golden snitch he had caught which is a clue upon finding the Horcruxes.

This simple yet spectacular Golden Snitch Cocktail is all you will need! With sweet, fruity, floral elderflower champagne flavors and shimmery gold luster swirls, this cocktail is a party on its own!

Ingredients

2 oz St-Germain liqueur (or fake it with mixture of 1 oz vodka and 1 oz elderflower cordial)
3 1/2 oz dry champagne (or sparkling wine)
1/4 tsp of gold luster dust
Serving: 1 Drink

- - -*- - -*- - -*- - -

Instructions

- Put St-Germain liqueur (or the mixture of vodka and elderflower cordial) into a bottle. Add gold luster dust to the mixture base and stir to make it shimmer.
- Pour this into a champagne flute, then top it with sparkling (preferably a sweeter sparkling wine like extra-dry or dry champagne, prosecco or a spumante)
- Repeat for as many glasses as you like!

Bonus: Non-Alcoholic Cocktail Version

Ingredients:
2 ounces elderflower drink concentrate
3 1/2 ounces sparkling water
1/4 tsp of gold luster dust

Instructions

Steps as above. Replace St-Germain liqueur with elderflower drink concentrate and sparkling wine with sparkling water.

Dumbledore Cocktail

Former Hogwarts students can recall visiting Albus Dumbledore's office and seeing a bowl on his desk filled to the brim with lemon drops. Everyone who knew the powerful headmaster knew his affinity for the sour candy that he simply couldn't resist. While concocting this sour drink named after the treat, we use fresh sugar from Honeydukes candy shop to coat the glass' rim, but any sugar will do.

*** This pungent drink, dedicated to the beloved headmaster, tastes both tart and refreshing, making it the perfect cocktail for adults with a sweet tooth!

Ingredients

4 oz vodka
1 oz triple sec
2 oz simple syrup
2 oz lemon juice
Lemon, for zesting

Tip: you can use any orange-flavored liquor to replace triple sec if you don't have it

Serving: 2-3 Drinks

Hey. I would like to order 1 Dumbledore cocktail please!

Instructions

-First, sugar the rim of your glass. Set aside. See "how to" instruction at the beginning of this book.

-In a cocktail shaker filled with ice, add the remaining ingredients. Attach lid and shake well.

-Zest or cut two small strips of lemon skin from your lemon, and then twist well. I find a chopstick is great for helping get a nice spiral, but you can just twist with your fingers. Garnish the glass with the lemon twist and serve.

Phoenix's Tear Cocktail

Phoenixes have crimson feathers on their body and a golden tail as long as a peacock's. Phoenix are extremely loyal creatures, and are capable of arriving to the aid of beings who share a similar devotion.

This was how Fawkes arrived to assist Harry in slaying the Basilisk in the Chamber of Secrets during his second year at Hogwarts. Their tears have potent healing capabilities. For instance, phoenix tears are the only known antidote to basilisk venom. This Cocktail is Guaranteed to perk you right up, even if you've been bitten by a Basilisk.

Ingredients

10 basil leaves, plus 1 basil leaf for garnish
Ice
3 ounces Lillet blanc
1/2 ounce gin
1 ounce Simple Syrup

Serving: 1-2 Drinks

Instructions

- In a cocktail shaker, lightly muddle the 10 basil leaves.
- Add ice and the Lillet, gin and Simple Syrup and shake well.
- Double strain into a chilled coupe and garnish with the remaining basil leaf.

"A gentle creature, the phoenix lives to an immense age because it can regenerate each time it bursts into flames. Phoenix song is magical and its tears have healing properties." —Chocolate Frog Card

Forbidden Forest Cocktail

The forest is a very old place that holds many secrets and houses many creatures. It is strictly off limits to students. Inspired by this historic forest, we add ingredient all down to the botanicals.

Gin is from the herbs, roots, and plants that lend the spirit their own distinct character. When we think of foraging, we think of green, and the near-endless number of vibrant green plants whose flavors are just waiting to be discovered.

Ingredients

5 long dandelion leaves
2 oz of gin (we like The Botanist most)
1 oz of fresh lime juice
3/4 oz of simple syrup
Ice

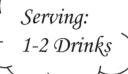

Serving:
1-2 Drinks

Instructions

In the bottom of a cocktail shaker, muddle long dandelion leaves (tearing them into quarters before you muddle). Add gin, fresh lime juice, simple syrup, and ice. Shake, hard, then double-strain into a rocks glass with fresh ice. Garnish with three dandelion leaves, torn down to the size you want.

Goblet of Fire Cocktail

This cocktail inspired by The Goblet of Fire which was the "impartial judge" for the Triwizard Tournament, who chose which students will represent their respective schools during the upcoming tasks of the tournament. The charming magic of the The Goblet of Fire is- of course: The fire. We have tailored a wonderful recipe which is quite simple to make even at home.

To make this cocktail far more different from other common flaming cocktails, why not give this Goblet of Fire Cocktail a little bit more sexier look with a "Hawaii" theme. Wizards also have fun and vacations, right?

* Remember, don't let it burn too long. You have to take your own responsibility playing with fire, our dear wizards.

Ingredients

2 ⅓ oz Dark Jamaican Rum
2 ⅔ oz Cream of Coconut
⅔ oz Fresh Lime Juice
Half a spent Lime Shell
1 Piece of Bread soaked in 151 Proof Rum
1 pinch Cinnamon

Serving:
1-2 Drinks

Instructions

-Add the dark rum, cream of coconut and lime juice into a blender, plus ice to roughly the level of the liquid. Blitz until slushy.

-Pour into a goblet.

-To garnish, hollow out your spent lime shell and float on the top. Take a piece of toasted bread or cracker, soak in 151-proof rum and place in your lime shell. Ignite with a long-stemmed match, stand well back and marvel at the ensuing display of fire.

-For a little extra theatre, throw a dash of cinnamon over the flames and watch the magic happen.

Felix Felicis (Liquid Luck)

Felix Felicis, more commonly known as Liquid Luck. This is a potion that when taken is said to imbue the user with impossibly good luck until the effects of the potion wear off and a bottle of it was given to Harry by Professor Slughorn for brewing a perfect potion in class.

This bottle of Liquid Luck ends up being a significant plot point in the book as Harry uses it against Slughorn to extract information. It is very difficult to make, disastrous if made wrong, and requires **six months** to stew before it is ready to be consumed. Today, you don't have to wait such long time.

Now, it takes you only about 5 minutes to make Liquid Luck with our recipe. Let's start and have some fun!

Ingredients

2 oz. London dry gin
1 tsp. superfine sugar
1/2 oz. lemon juice
5 oz. brut champagne

*** Serving: 2-3 Drinks

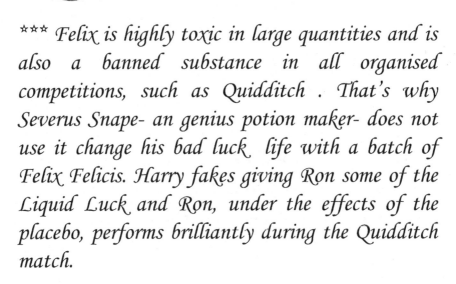

Instructions

Shake gin, lemon juice, and sugar well with cracked ice in a chilled cocktail shaker. Strain into a glass and top off with champagne.

*** Felix is highly toxic in large quantities and is also a banned substance in all organised competitions, such as Quidditch . That's why Severus Snape- an genius potion maker- does not use it change his bad luck life with a batch of Felix Felicis. Harry fakes giving Ron some of the Liquid Luck and Ron, under the effects of the placebo, performs brilliantly during the Quidditch match.

Flaming Dragon Cocktail

In harry Potter, dragons are giant winged, fire-breathing reptilian beasts. Widely regarded as terrifying yet awe-inspiring, they can be found all over the world and are frequently referred to in Asian and medieval European folklore. Dragon is one of the most dangerous and hardest to conceal creatures in the wizarding world.

This fabulous cocktail has ingredients that are easy to put together but delicious, and a show-stopper at any party. You will love the look, the taste and the theatrics – a sure-fire way.

Ingredients

2 oz Bacardi Superior rum
1.5 oz raspberry syrup
¾ oz freshly squeezed lemon juice 2 ice cubes
⅛ tsp of white luster dust or red luster dust (Optional)
2 tsp Bacardi rum 151

Serving: 1-2 Drinks

Instructions

Place all the ingredients in a cocktail mixer (luster dust as well, if you want a shimmery cocktail).

Shake for a few second to chill the cocktail. Strain the cocktail into a coupe glass.

Place a cocktail spoon over the surface of the cocktail and carefully layer the rum 151 over the cocktail. Litter right before serving and watch the magic.

* Please do remember to blow out the flame.

Sirius Black Cocktail

Sirius Black, also known as Padfoot or Snuffles (in his Animagus form) was an English pure-blood wizard, the older son of Orion and Walburga Black. Although he was the heir of the House of Black, He was the black sheep of his family about belief in blood purity and defied tradition.

"We've all got both light and dark inside us. What matters is the part we choose to act on. That's who we really are."- Sirius Black

This cocktail is designed based on the characters of Sirius Black , the God father of Harry Potter. Despite fallen leaves and cooler temperatures, this black rum and sugar cocktail will have you seeing palm trees.

Ingredients

1 ½ oz black rum
3/4 oz crème de cacao
1 cup ice Black food color
1 tablespoon brown sugar

Serving: 1 Drink

Instructions

- Add black rum, crème de cacao, ice and 1 or 2 drops black food color to a martini shaker.
- In small bowl, add brown sugar and 1 drop black food color. Mix with fork until all sugar is black. Wet rim of martini glass with water. Dip rim into sugar.
- Strain martini into glass, and serve.

Tip: To get the sugar to stick better to the martini glass, use corn syrup or honey instead of water before dipping into black sugar.

Hermione Sunrise Cocktail

Hermione first met Harry Potter and Ron Weasley aboard the Hogwarts Express. She was often described to be to be "the brightest witch of her age". Hermione played a significant role in many other battles of the Second Wizarding War. In 1997, she fought in the Battle of the Seven Potters, alongside the Order of the Phoenix. The trio do everything together and everything can't be done without our lovely talented girl.

Why not treat her a cocktail named following her. Master the art of a classic tequila based cocktail and have fun with your friends.

Ingredients

2 tsp grenadine; Ice
1.6 oz tequila
1 tbsp triple sec
1 large orange or 2 small ones, juiced
½ lemon, juiced
1 cocktail cherry

**Serving:
1 Drink**

Instructions

- Pour the grenadine into the base of a tall glass and set aside. Fill a cocktail shaker with ice and add the tequila, triple sec and fruit juices. Shake until the outside of the shaker feels cold.
- Add a few ice cubes to the serving glass then carefully double strain the cocktail into it, trying not to disturb the grenadine layer too much. Add more ice if needed to fill the glass then garnish with a cherry on a stick or cocktail umbrella.

Bellatrix Cocktail

In Harry Potter Series, Bellatrix Lestrange (née Black) was an English pure-blood Dark witch. She was a member of the House of Black, an old wizarding family. When starting education at Hogwarts, Bellatrix was Sorted into Slytherin House. After graduating from Hogwarts, Bellatrix became a Death Eater. She was fanatically loyal to Lord Voldemort and was among the most dangerous and sadistic of his followers. Bellatrix was an intensely sadistic witch with brutal, violent tendencies.

To make a Cocktail named after her, I thought of something very very dark so I chose black color and using black licorice rope for garnishing.

If you're not a fan of black licorice, this is the most horrifying cocktail you could drink. If you're a lover of Jaeger, you'll find it scary delicious. Blueberry pomegranate juice shaken with black vodka and Jägermeister then garnished with black widow "legs" is utterly to-die for!

Serving: 1 Drink

Ingredients

2 ounces black vodka
1 ounce Jägermeister
1 ounce blueberry pomegranate juice
Garnish: Black licorice rope

Instructions

- Shake the ingredients with ice in a cocktail shaker and strain the mixture into a martini glass.
- Garnish with 4 black licorice rope pieces cut into 3-4 inch long "legs" on each side.

Dobby The Happy Elf Cocktail

Dobby was a male house-elf who served the Malfoy family. Harry tricked Lucius Malfoy into freeing Dobby. Dobby's new happy life nearby his closest friends: Harry, Ron, and Hermione. Dobby helped Harry spy on Draco Malfoy. Dobby went on Aberforth Dumbledore's orders to save the lives of Harry and his companions from Death Eaters at Malfoy Manor.

During this rescue he was fatally wounded by Bellatrix Lestrange's knife. At the beach, Dobby smiled and passed away in Harry's arms. If Dobby were alive, he surely wants to celebrate and share the joy with his friends after victory of the battle against Vodermort. This recipe delicated to Dobby and his friends.

Ingredients

1 medium lime, cut in half
Granulated sugar
24 oz (3 cups)crushed ice
8 oz (1 cup) tequila
2 tablespoons powdered sugar
½ can (12-ounce size) frozen peach juice concentrate, thawed
6 peach slices

Serving: 6 Drinks

Instructions

Rub rims of 6 stemmed glasses with 1 lime half; dip rims of glasses into granulated sugar.

Squeeze juice from both lime halves into blender. Add remaining ingredients except peach slices to blender. Cover and blend on high speed until foamy. Pour into glasses. Garnish sides of glasses with peach slices. Serve immediately.

Tip: Pour leftover peach juice concentrate into ice-cube trays and freeze. The ice cubes will jazz up iced tea, lemonade or even club soda.

Firewhisky Cocktail

There is a minimum drinking age higher than 17 in JKR's novels. This rule is not always followed. In The Deathly Hallows, Harry gets his first taste of firewhisky, toasting the memory of fallen hero Alastor Moody. Serve this up neat when courage is needed, or mix it with a bit of ginger ale for a tasty but less fiery cocktail suitable for parties. Served in the Hog's Head pub, this concoction is for the bravest wizard and/or witch.

In wizarding world, popular Firewhiskey brands include Ogden's Old Firewhisky and Blishen's Firewhisky. It is known to cause a burning sensation when drunk, and for filling one's body with courage. If you are brave enough and wish to try, I'll show you how in no time.

Ingredients
1 oz of whiskey
1/2 oz of cinnamon schnapps
1 Splash of 151 rum
Serving: 1 Drink

Instructions
Add whiskey and cinnamon schnapps to shaker with ice. Shake to chill, then pour into shot glass. Lastly, use layering technique to add 151 rum on the top and ignite.

Note: PLEASE blow out before drinking.

"Ron Weasley commented that he could most likely purchase Firewhisky at the Hog's Head during the Dumbledore's Army meeting. Hermione was angered at that, furiously reminding him of his prefect status. He instead had Butterbeer."

Chocolatini Wolfbane Cocktail

The Wolfsbane Potion was an innovative and complex potion that relieves, but does not cure, the symptoms of lycanthropy, or werewolfry . Contrary to the bad taste of the real Wolfbane, This Chocolatini Wolfbane Cocktail wll please Remus Lupin or any of our chocolate lovers.

Ingredients

3 oz irish cream
2 oz vodka
1 oz Crème de Cacao
Ice cubes

Serving: 1 Drink

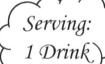

Instructions

Fill up the shaker with ice pour Crème de Cacao vodka and irish cream into the shaker. Shake well. Strain into the cocktail glass garnish with ground chocolate

Lumos Cocktail

The Wand-Lighting Charm (Lumos) is a charm that illuminates the tip of the caster's wand. Perfect for bed time reading or sneaking around at night. So many activities. It is commonly used in Harry Potter series and is one of the favourite spells of many Harry Potter nerds. Lumos Cocktail is a simple classic cocktail featuring rum, lime and simple syrup. You can tweak the ingredient ratio to your taste just as you can modify the light volume as you want with Lumos or Mumos Maxima.

Ingredients

2 oz light rum
Juice of 1/2 lime or lemon
1/4 ounce simple syrup
(or 1 tsp powdered sugar)
Garnish: 1 Lime slice

Serving: 1 drink

Instructions

Pour everything into a cocktail shaker with ice. Shake until chilled.

Strain the mixture into a chilled cocktail glass. Garnish with a lime piece.

PolyJuice Potion Punch

Polyjuice Potion is a potion that allows the drinker to assume the form of someone else. It is a highly complicated, challenging and time-consuming potion that even adult witches and wizards struggle to brew correctly. Today we're going to make a **PolyJuice Potion Cocktail** with much less effort. To have "witchy" look, we've choosen green theme for this cocktail.

This cocktail is served in a pint glass or any specific big glass you have. I'm sorry to say that you will not turn into a different person by drinking this version, unless of course you drink too much.

Ingredients
* Two .13-ounce packets unsweetened lemon-lime drink mix, such as Kool-Aid
* 2 cups sugar
* One 46-ounce can pineapple juice
* 12 oz frozen lemonade concentrate, thawed
* 32 oz ginger ale
* Yield: 1 gallon

Instructions
Put 2 quarts water in a 1 gallon container. Add the drink mix and sugar and stir until the sugar is dissolved. Add the pineapple juice and lemonade concentrate and stir well. Just before serving, add the ginger ale.

Notes
Dry Ice is a fun, and easy way to create a fun party with special fog effects. The idea of making a Cauldron Brew Dry Ice Punch for a witch theme party make it feel especially festive. Use dry ice with your own risk because it's -78 degree Celsius which is very cold and poses risk for instant frost-bite on bare skin.

Things you'll need to make a *foggy dry ice punch bowl*:
- A large bowl for the dry ice
- A smaller bowl for the punch
- Hot water
- Dry ice

Instructions:
- Place an empty punch bowl into a large container (picture 2) then add punch to the punch bowl, add dry ice into the large bowl around your punch bowl (picture 3). Make sure you never touch the dry ice directly as it is very cold.
- Pour hot water into the dry ice. As the water cools, add more hot water to maintain the fog effect. As a rule of thumb, one kg of dry ice will create 5-6 minutes of fog effect.
- You can also use a cauldron as the larger container outside to have a more witchy look for your party.

Pink Tonk Warrior Gin

Nymphadora Tonks, more commonly known as Tonks, was an Auror trained by Alastor Moody. Tonks and Remus were married in the summer of 1997. She formed part of the Advance Guard and bravely participated in the Battle of the Seven Potters. She was was finally murdered by Bellatrix Lestrange in the Battle of Hogwarts. She gave birth to a son, Teddy Remus Lupin. After her death, her son was raised by her mother and Harry. This cocktail is Inspried by Tonk's pink hair along side with her positive and humorous character.

Ingredients
2 oz The Bitter Truth Pink Gin
0.5 oz pink peppercorn simple syrup
2 strawberries (muddled and strained)
1 bar-spoon Green Chartreuse
Serving: 1 drink
Instructions
Combine all ingredients. Pour into martini glass. Garnish with rosemary sprig.

Harry's Scar Cocktail

The iconic lightning bolt scar on Harry Potter's forehead is the result of a failed murder attempt by Lord Voldemort. His mother's loving sacrifice protected him. The incident also inadvertently made Harry into a Horcrux, as a piece of the Dark Lord's soul embedded itself in Harry. Harry's scar hurt whenever Voldemort was close or experiencing strong negative emotions. It looks like a lightning bolt but in fact, it's shape is the hand motion for casting the Avada Kedavra spell.

I am a Potterhead who will never grow tire of making new recipes from the superb series. I've known and belonged to the magic that is Harry Potter. A cocktail named after the legendary scar Cocktail would be a very nice try.

Ingredients

1 ½ oz. Arette tequila
½ oz. Vida mezcal
¾ oz. Blood orange juice
½ oz. Lime juice
½ oz. Bonal gentiane quina
½ oz. Agave syrup (cut with half water)

Instructions

Combine ingredients in mixing glass and shake. Pour into rocks glass that's been rimmed with maca, dehydrated citrus and smoked salt. Garnish with a blood orange wheel

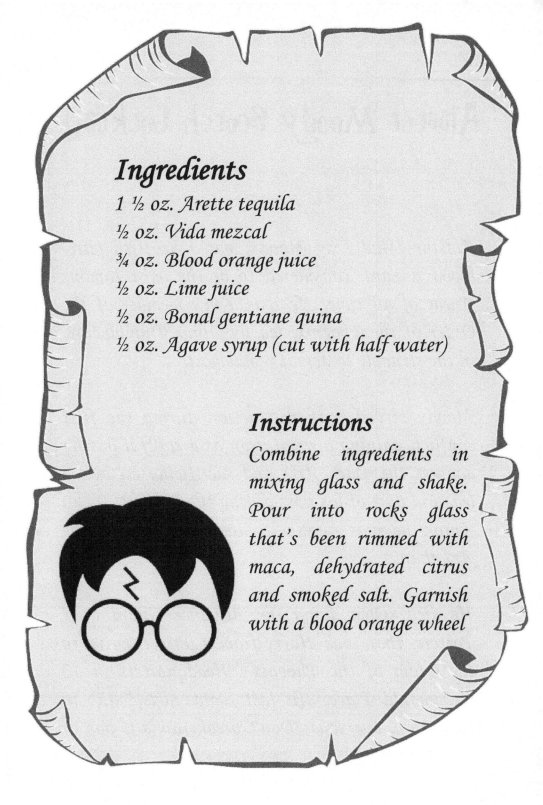

Alastor Moody Scotch Cocktail

Alastor "Mad-Eye" Moody was a Scottish pure-blood wizard, considered to be the most famous Auror of all time. He was a key member of the Order of the Phoenix, led by Albus Dumbledore, in the struggle to defeat Voldemort.

Moody served with distinction during the first conflict, gaining a reputation as a skillful battler against the Dark Arts and sacrificing an eye, a leg, and part of his nose during the conflict. As an Auror, he was known to imprison half of The Azkaban.

He died when doing the Advance Guard of 7 Potters, that took Harry from 4 Privet Drive to the Order of the Phoenix's Headquarters in 12 Grimmauld Place. His last words was "Stay in formation, everyone. Don't break ranks if one of us gets killed."

Scotch is used as the base of this cocktail although isn't the most common spirit for cocktails, which reminds us about Alastor Moody, a Scottish wizard with a unique characteristic and look.

Ingredients

1 oz Ardbeg Ten Years Old scotch
1 1/2 oz Pür Likör spice blood orange liqueur
1/2 oz Fresh lime juice
1/2 oz Apple butter
3 dashesFee Brothers Aztec chocolate bitters

Instructions

Combine all the ingredients in a shaker with ice, and shake until appropriately diluted and chilled.

Fine-strain into a chilled coupe glass, and garnish with 1 or 2 dehydrated lime wheels floating on top.

Amortentia Potion Cocktail

The tickled pink cocktail is a perfectly simple drink recipe that's sure to impress anyone. This Harry Potter-inspired love potion is a magical mixed drink that's perfect for Valentine's Day, anniversaries, or anytime you want to express affection to your heart's desire. When you whip up a batch of these boozy brews, you'll both start feeling a little bewitched!

"Amortentia" is the most powerful love potion in existence. "It is distinctive for its mother-of-pearl sheen, and steam rises from the potion in spirals." In Latin, amor means "love," and this brew is basically liquid infatuation!

Ingredients

2 oz cranberry juice, Ice
¾ oz lime juice
1½ oz London dry gin
¾ oz rosemary simple syrup
4 oz soda water
Rosemary sprig for garnish
Pearl Dust and Cranberries for garnish

Serving: 1 Drink

Instructions

- In a cocktail shaker, combine the cranberry juice, lime juice, gin, and syrup. Add the ice and shake.
- Strain into a collins glass filled with ice. Add the soda water. Stir.
- Garnish with a sprig of rosemary and cranberries.
- For best shimmery effect, mix the pearl dust in after shaking.

Veritaserum Cocktail

Veritaserum is a Potion discribed to effectively force the drinker answering any questions put to them truthfully, though there are certain methods of resistance. Using Veritaserum on a student was strictly forbidden, at least in Hogwarts but Dolores Umbridge used many times on Hogwarts' students when she was in charged. In the magic world, it sounds like a very dangerous drink. Here's a fun cocktail twist on the intimidating Veritaserum!

This cocktail is less scary than the real potion but be careful, Brandy and amaretto liqueur are a deadly combo that'll "have you spilling your innermost secrets" if you have too many!

Ingredients

White sugar crystals
4 oz vanilla ice cream
1 oz brandy
1 oz amaretto liqueur
1/4 teaspoon ground nutmeg
1 oz vanilla ice cream
Pumpkin pie spice, for garnish

Serving: 1 Drink

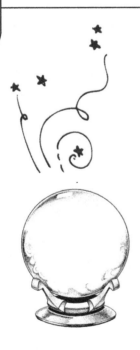

Instructions

Spread some sugar crystals in a saucer. Dampen rims of martini glasses and coat with sugar crystals. Combine the eggnog, brandy, amaretto, nutmeg, and vanilla ice cream in a blender. Pour into prepare martini glasses. Garnish each drink with a pinch of pumpkin pie spice.

Expecto Patronum Cocktail

The Patronus Charm (Expecto Patronum) is the most famous and one of the most powerful defensive charms known to wizardkind. It'san extremely difficult spell, that evokes a partially-tangible positive energy force known as a Patronus.

If you want an absolutely perfect drink for reminding good memories, look no further! This half sweet, half sour and 100% refreshing cocktail is the best potion you can find. The visually appealing blue lagoon cocktail is an easy and delicious beverage to make. In fact, it requires only three ingredients and a garnish. Also, it's blue color makes it perfect for keeping the Dementors away.

Ingredients

Lime wedge , Ice cubes
Coarse sugar or granulated sugar
¼ cup cranberry juice cocktail
1 oz citron vodka or vodka
1 oz blue curacao
1 tablespoon fresh lime juice

Serving: 1 Drink

Instructions

- Moisten rim of chilled martini glass with lime wedge. Sprinkle sugar onto small plate, and dip moistened rim into the sugar to coat lightly.
- Fill cocktail shaker with ice. Add cranberry juice, vodka, curacao and lime juice; cover and shake. Strain into martini glass.

Avada Bombastic Cocktail

The Killing Curse (Avada Kedavra) is the most powerful and sinister spells known to Wizardkind. This curse was mostly used by Vodermort and Death Eaters. With this cocktail, I use a green color to describe "flash of blinding green light" and also throw a little "blood" into it! In Harry Potter Series, when cast successfully on a living person or creature the curse causes a death, without any injury to the body, and without any trace of violence. The idea of ganishing with "bloody" theme is just for fun. Avada Punch Cocktail is actually a shot- a strong and crazy shot.

It's akin to moonshine in its strength so be careful! One or two will pack a powerful punch! This is simple to make, and people will think you worked harder than you actually did.

Gotta love that!

Ingredients

1 Part Irish cream
2 Parts Melon Liqueur
1 Splash Blue Curacao Syrup
(or any home made Simple Syrup)

Serving:
1 drink

Instructions

-Pour melon liqueur into shot glass and gently layer Irish cream on top.
-Drop blue curacao syrup inside. Green Apple Simple Syrup
-Blood for the rims or put a drop or two into the shot just before people tilt it back for a cool effect. This blood is sticky sweet and simply made with red food coloring and corn syrup

Bonus: How to make Apple Simple Syrup

Grab apples, chop them up, throw them in a pot with water and Granulated Sugar, then bring it to a boil. Mash it up, strain it and Let it cool.

Alohomora Cocktail

The Unlocking Charm (Alohomora), is a charm that unlocks objects such as doors or windows. Hermione used it to open a forbidden entrance on the Third-floor corridor of Hogwarts Castle before the admiring eyes of Harry and Ron.

Alohomora is a cocktail with its own cheer; you'll shout its name upon tasting! A refreshing, fruity concoction with added bubbles, it's elegant and sophisticated—just like you can open all doors. Alohomora!

Ingredients

1 oz Apple Brandy of choice
1 oz Apple Juice
Champagne to fill
Spring of Mint

Serving: 1 drink

Instructions

Add Apple brandy and mint to a old fashioned tumbler glass, mashing the two to mix and bruise leaves. Fill with ice, then pour over apple juice. Top to brim with Champagne, garnish with mint

Bonus: A tumbler is a flat-bottomed beverage container usually made of plastic or glass. Old Fashioned tumbler glass, traditionally used for a simple cocktail or liquor "on the rocks" (alcohol, served in a glass with ice cubes.).

Wine Glass

Champagne Flute Glass

Pint Glass

Tumbler Glass

*Some kinds of cocktail glasses

Gillywater Cocktail

Gillywater is an alcoholic beverage that Professor Minerva McGonagall and Luna Lovegood ordered at the The Three Broomsticks, and Romilda Vane once tried to convince Harry Potter to drink some that she had spiked with Love Potion. It's more likely that Gillywater is related to the magical plant Gillyweed which Harry Potter consumes in order to win the second round of the TriWizard Tournament.

> In the books, Gillyweed is described as bundles of slimy, grey-green rat tails. Grown organically, the flowers are entirely edible. To make the copy of Gilly Weed, I actually put a fresh looking on it. Although it looks simple, it tastes really good.

Ingredients

5 ounces Coconut Vodka (or tequila)
2 tsp lime juice
2 tsp lemon juice
Coconut water, Ice
Simple syrup – optional
Garnish: Lime slices, Lemon slices
Serving: 2 drinks

Instructions

In a cocktail shaker combine the vodka and citrus juices and shake well.

Fill two tall collins glasses with ice layering a few lemon and lime slices with the ice. Divide the vodka between the glasses and then top each glass with coconut water.

Stir slightly and serve

Tips:

This cocktail is awesome with just lemons or just limes or even a little orange juice/orange slices. If you prefer sweeter - add in a little simple syrup - about one teaspoon to each cocktail. This cocktail is also really good with 1800 coconut tequila, which I might even prefer over the vodka.

Gryffindor Lion Cocktail

Gryffindor is one of the four Houses of Hogwarts School of Witchcraft and Wizardry and was founded by Godric Gryffindor. Gryffindor instructed the Sorting Hat to choose students possessing characteristics he most valued, such as courage, chivalry, and determination[, to be sorted into his house.. Gryffindor corresponds roughly to the element of fire and the emblematic animal is a lion. Gryffindor house contributed many members to Dumbledore's Army and the Order of the Phoenix.

All sophisticated Harry Potters and Gryffindors' fan will answer to this cocktail! This gin and Marnier based citrusy cocktail is dibiberately and indeed originally, formulated to be tad on the sour side, bit is balanced by a suger crusted rim.

Ingredients

1½ oz dry gin
¾ oz grand manier liquer
¾ oz freshly squeezed orange juice
¼ oz freshly squeezed lemon juice
1/6 oz pomegranate syrup
1 dash orange bitter
Ice

Serving: 1 drink

Instructions

Add ice to the shaker
Add all ingredients and ice to the shaker, shake well

Garnish: Rub around the rim of a chilled cocktail glass with orange juice or syrup. Roll the rim of the cocktail glass in the sugar.

I use coupe glass for serving this cocktail.

Ravenclaw Cocktail

Ravenclaw is one of the four Houses of Hogwarts School of Witchcraft and Wizardry. Its founder was the medieval witch Rowena Ravenclaw. Members of this house are characterised by their wit, learning, and wisdom. Intensely intelligent, Ravenclaws are also unique and think outside the box. Luna Lovewood is an example, she gave Harry a hint about the Lost Diadem of Ravenclaw which was lost for centuries before it became a Horcrux. Or another Ravenclaw: Garrick Ollivander, he possessed an eidetic memory and can remember every wand he has sold.

One simple addition turns your dry gin martini into a slightly fruity, blue delight of the Ravenclaw House's Color. Blue curaçao is the key ingredient in the Sapphire Martini and just a couple dashes do the trick.

To The Ravenclaws!

Ingredients

4 parts gin (Bombay Sapphire or other premium gin, frozen), Ice
1 part blue curacao
1 dash dry vermouth (optional)
Garnish: maraschino cherry (optional)

This martini is written like a standard drink recipe, meaning that instead of an exact measurement (ex: 1 cup) the recipe will read "1 part." For example, let's say you wanted to make one drink – this typically means you're using 1 standard shot glass for measuring. So then when the recipe says "1 part" you would interpret that amount as "1 standard shot glass" full. If the recipe says "1/2 part" you'd fill the shot glass halfway so that it's "1/2 standard shot glass." OR, let's say you wanted to make enough drinks for a few friends. When making the drink you could interpret "1 part" as "1 cup" (or "1/2 part" to "1/2 cup.")

Instructions

-In a cocktail shaker filled with ice, add gin, blue curacao, and dry vermouth (optional). Shake vigorously until combined.

-Strain sapphire martini into a martini glass. Garnish with lemon, orange, or a maraschino cherry

Slytherin Cocktail

Slytherin is one of the four houses of Hogwarts School of Witchcraft and Wizardry and was founded by Salazar Slytherin. Slytherins are known for being cunning and ambitious, although it is also known to have produced many Dark witches and wizards. According to J.K. Rowling, Slytherin roughly corresponds to the element of water. Slytherins are associated with cunning, ambition and are always striving to be the best. However, Slytherins will never leave their own behind.

The Slytherin Cocktail recipe is incredibly easy, focusing primarily on gin and adding just a hint of green crème de menthe. You want to be careful about adding too much mint because it will overpower the gin and knock the drink out of balance.

Ingredients

1 1/2 ounces gin
1 teaspoon green crème de menthe
2 dashes bitters

Instructions

- Gather the ingredients, pour the ingredients into a cocktail shaker filled with ice cubes. Shake well.
- Strain into a chilled cocktail glass.
- Serve and enjoy!

Tips:

The Emerald Isle recipe doesn't specify which bitters to use. A good default is aromatic bitters, such as Angostura, though mint bitters make an equally nice complement. If you're feeling a little wild, orange bitters are quite interesting for the palate as well.

Green crème de menthe is preferred over the white (clear) version because of the color it brings to the drink. However, you can pour white crème de menthe and enjoy the exact same taste.

Hufflepuff Brew Party Cocktail

Hufflepuff is known for having members that are patient, fair, hard-working, and sometimes blandly nice. Among the four Hogwarts houses in the Harry Potter series by J.K. Rowling, Hufflepuff is sometimes perceived as being a miscellaneous category. Hufflepuff can also denote someone or something that's not particularly memorable, with no notable characteristics. But J.K. Rowling, herself, to make a statement that Hufflepuff is just as admirable a house as any other. Hufflepuff (yellow and black, representing wheat and soil) is connected to earth.

As stunning as it is delicious, this Hufflepuff Cocktail is as friendly as Hufflepuffs. Not incredibly strong, it's more of a party punch type of drink where your guests can enjoy them all night long without getting sloshed.

Ingredients

2 1/2 oz Midori melon liqueur
2 1/2 oz lemon lime soda (I use Sprite)
2 1/2 oz orange juice
Garnish: Black sugar, Simple Syrup
Serving: *1 Drink*

Instructions

-Add black sanding sugar to a small plate, and light corn syrup to another small plate. Dip rims of martini glasses in corn syrup, then into sanding sugar.

-Add ice to a cocktail shaker and pour ingredients in. Shake until chilled, then pour into martini glasses and serve.

Bonus: *To make non-alcoholic, use 3 1/2 oz orange juice and 4 oz lemon lime soda, then add a few drops of yellow food coloring*

Note: *I serve this drink in my martini glasses, which hold 8 oz, but you can definitely serve them in any glass you'd like.*

Quidditch Worldcup Cocktail

The Quidditch World Cup has been held every four years. In "Harry Potter and the Goblet of Fire" it's described as "A source of vehement disagreements, a security risk for all who attend it and a frequent focus for unrest and protest, the Quidditch World Cup is simultaneously the most exhilarating sporting event on earth and a logistical nightmare for the host nation."

Quiditch Cup Cocktail is both a liqueur and a mixed drink. It is a delightful and easy beverage that pairs the namesake liqueur with lemonade and it may quickly become one of your new favorites.

Quiditch Cup Cocktail is designed to be the 'official' refreshment of Quiditch Worldcup.

Ingredients
1 part Pimm's Cup No. 1
3 parts lemonade
Garnish: mint, orange, and/or strawberries
Garnish: cucumber slice or peel

Instructions
Pour the liqueur into a collins glass filled with ice cubes. Add the lemonade. Garnish with the cucumber and any combination of mint, orange, or strawberries. Serve and enjoy!

* The liqueur featured is Pimm's Cup No. 1, a gin-based spirit liqueur with a deep red color that is flavored with 'herbal botanicals,' spices, and caramelized orange.

*Fun Fact: In the book Harry Potter and The Goblet of Fire, we first read about the Portkey. Harry go with Ron, Mr Weasly, Cedric and Cedric's father using a portkey going to the Quidditch World cup. Portkey is a magical object enchanted to instantly bring anyone touching it to a specific location. Most of the time, a Portkey is an everyday object that would not draw the attention of a Muggle.

Cocktail name:......................

Ingredients

Instructions

Cocktail name:.........................

Ingredients

Instructions

Cocktail name: ....

Ingredients

....
....
....
....
....
....

Instructions

....
....
....
....
....
....
....
....

Cocktail name: ....

Ingredients

....
....
....
....
....
....

Instructions

....
....
....
....
....
....
....
....

Cocktail name:.........................

Ingredients

Instructions

Cocktail name:.....................

Ingredients

....
....
....
....
....
....

Instructions

....
....
....
....
....
....
....
....

Cocktail name:...........................

Ingredients

Instructions

Cocktail name:............................

Ingredients

Instructions

Cocktail name: . . . .

Ingredients

Instructions

Made in the USA
Monee, IL
10 December 2020